The Funeral:
An Endangered Tradition – Making Sense of the Final Farewell

Johnette Hartnett

Published by Good Mourning, P.O. 9355, South Burlington, VT
05407-9355; distributed by same.

ISBN: 1-883171-98-9 (Volume 3)
ISBN: 1-883171-81-4 (6 Volume Set)
Library of Congress Catalog Card Number: 93-90776

The Good Mourning Series has been partially funded by a grant
from the National Funeral Directors Association (NFDA).

This book is dedicated to my three cherubs,
as I so often called them.

DAVID JOHN
July 4, 1971 - March 8, 1983

JOHNETTE THERESE
December 19, 1972 - March 8, 1983

JOHN PETER
May 28, 1974 - March 8, 1983

*All your past except its beauty is gone,
and nothing is left but a blessing.*
                                    – A Course in Miracles

The Funeral:
An Endangered Tradition –
Making Sense of the Final Farewell

Contents

Foreword

On March 8, 1983, my three children and housekeeper died in a fire in St. Albans, Vermont. My son David John was eleven years old; my daughter, Johnette Therese, was nine; and my son John Peter was eight. Our housekeeper, Nancy, was twenty-one.

Until that day I was a busy and happy woman. Although I was facing a divorce, my life was full with children, a busy professional career and rewarding community work.

Until that day, I belonged to an elite and extremely fortunate group of people to whom such tragedies simply did not happen. We lived in an idyllic small New England town, conspicuously and deliberately lacking the traffic, crime and social ills that plague big cities. We watched those things happen to other people in the movies and on TV or in the newspapers. In our insulated, tight-knit community, we were protected. We were financially secure and the children were healthy, intelligent, talented and athletic. Nothing could happen to us.

Then in the spark of a smoldering ember, our defenses failed, the plan to keep us safe from unspeakable horror disintegrated, and the unimaginable became a reality.

Not one, but all three of my children died. Together. Of smoke inhalation.

The effects, I probably do not need to tell you, have been excruciating, deep and lasting. During the first five years following the fire, I spent many, many hours in therapy sorting out the sometimes sordid events that led to and followed the tragedy. My therapy included sessions with three different professionals whose unique perspectives offered valuable guidance and counsel at different stages of my grief.

In addition to seeking professional help, I amassed a personal arsenal to guard against the waves of pain that to this day rise and subside in a sometimes destructive, sometimes therapeutic sea of sadness.

I have aggressively sought out detailed information on grief and the painful aftermath of death. In the past ten years, I have collected a library of research and attended countless seminars, workshops and professional-level courses. I've spent long hours among practitioners in the fields of mental health, grief, funeral and health-care. Through widening ripples of friendships and business associates, I have met, counseled and learned from others who have lost loved ones and who are searching for the same solace I seek.

Freud said that grief is a natural response to loss. I believe that Freud and his modern successors do not go far enough. For many people who have never experienced a loss, this "natural response" certainly seems like anything *but* natural or normal when it happens to you.

Cultural changes that have taken place over the last fifty to one hundred years have made grief all the more unnatural: Strong religious and community ties, close family units, well-preserved ceremonies and traditions used to lend unfailing support to bereaved families and friends. So many of those traditions have fallen by the wayside. As a culture we have handed over the care of our dying, our aged and our dead to institutions. A century ago, eighty percent of Americans died at home; today, eighty percent die in institutions. We are ignoring death until it hits us squarely in the face. Even then, we are trying to pretend it doesn't happen: Many cremations and burials take place without a funeral or memorial service of any kind.

At the same time, funeral directors are reporting a revealing and rather sad trend: Because funeral professionals are the only association many bereaved people have with death, grieving family members are drifting back to funeral homes for grief support, months after the deaths of their loved ones.

Not only do we lack knowledge of what to do, how to act or how to resolve grief issues for ourselves, we are also adrift and uncomfortable when faced with friends and acquaintances who are grieving. Amazingly, while I struggled with my grief, friends slowly dropped out of my life. The overprotective remark I always got when I asked, "Why? Why doesn't So-and-So call?" was, "You must understand, Johnette, people just don't know what to do or say." I would wonder how these people thought *I* would handle losing my whole family. I had never lost a whole family before. I didn't understand how to do it. I often found myself comforting *others* because of my loss. I became the expert on how to survive tragedy. In order to survive I had to teach others about loss.

Finally, like many people valiantly paddling in the wake of tragedy and grief, I have come to believe that perhaps the only way to make sense of the chaos is to help others. While many people are blessed with an innate ability to communicate compassion and strength and perspective in the presence of the bereaved, many more people are not so blessed.

I have seen a dire need to help people identify, understand and prepare for the process of grief.

The Funeral: An Endangered Tradition—Making Sense of the Final Farewell is the third in a series of six books I have written to address some of the most common issues I've come across in my recovery and in my research.

The entire series includes:

1. *Using Grief to Grow: A Primer*
   How You Can Help/How to Get Help

2. *Different Losses Different Issues:*
   What to Expect and How to Help.

3. *The Funeral: An Endangered Tradition*
   Making Sense of the Final Farewell

4. *Grief in the Workplace:*
   40 Hours Plus Overtime

5. *Children and Grief:*
   Big Issues for Little Hearts

6. *Death Etiquette for the '90s:*
   What to Do/What to Say

These books are written in an easy-to-pick-up, browse and digest, question-and-answer format. I have attempted to be complete without being overwhelming.

Some issues are supplemented with supporting anecdotes, separated from the rest of the text by this symbol: ❧.

In addition, I refer throughout the text to my other books, which may expand on questions of particular interest to you.

Please accept my sincere hope that you and the bereaved person you are concerned about will benefit from these practical, sensible books.

Johnette Hartnett
Burlington, VT 1993

The Funeral:
An Endangered Tradition –
Making Sense of the Final Farewell

Introduction

A popular but somewhat disturbing trend sees Americans deciding to skip the traditional funeral and opting for little or no funeral service at all. Of the two million-plus people who die in this country each year, about one third are cremated. Many of these cremations involve shortcuts in the traditional funeral service. The effect is not felt by the deceased, obviously, but by the living. An abbreviated funeral means the bereaved doesn't get prime time for grieving. The value of the American funeral has always been recognized as a time to show respect to the deceased and to give the living an opportunity to mourn publicly. This basic premise still holds, regardless of how we decide "to do" our funerals.

The trend to dismiss this tradition may have some long-range psychological effects on the bereaved that are not immediately obvious. One of the effects of skipping the whole business of a funeral service is that it leaves everyone with

7

empty time to fill instead of providing structured mourning time. Some people who scattered the ashes of their loved ones wish two years later they had not. "Family Only" funerals are becoming vogue.

The obvious (but often reluctant) reasons given for sidestepping the "traditional funeral" are, in part economic. In reality, the emotional and psychological costs of not grieving will far outweigh the monetary costs of a funeral.

The concept of building a business around death is somewhat difficult for many people to grasp. We have stigmatized anyone "in the business" because it just doesn't sound right to make money on death.

A rather complex problem emerges when we combine this trend with the fact that our culture is moving away from a sense of community-building and other traditional values. The bereaved suffer an increase in substance abuse, divorce rate, unemployment, and suicide. More and more bereaved are returning to the funeral homes looking for solace and help with their grief. The funeral industry is beginning to address this issue with "aftercare" programs for the bereaved. More funerals are beginning to be personalized and tailored to meet the changing demands of the American public (from videotaping to simple but meaningful services). Fifty years ago these people probably didn't need such unusual services from their undertaker, because they received comfort from relatives, neighbors, and churches. It's not unlikely that we will see legislation and funding to provide free grief support for this growing population in the near future.

Many people still refer to Jessica Mitford's book *The American Way of Death* as a guide to the current funeral industry, although it was published twenty-five years ago. Mitford's book opened funeral services up to public and Federal Trade Commission scrutiny and brought about many positive changes. Just because this industry deals with the sensitive issue of death does not exempt it from normal business abuses that may exist in any five-billion dollar industry.

We carry medical insurance in case of medical catastrophe, but until recently we didn't think of funerals as being in the same league. However, the cost of the average American funeral today is more than four thousand dollars (not including cemetery plot or marker). For many people this represents a difficult financial

burden. The funeral industry is just
beginning the process of educating the
public on pre-planning funerals. How
many people under the age of sixty-five
have ever thought about looking at these
future needs? How many people have
visited a funeral home in a non-grief time
for general information on what goes on
when a death occurs? How many people
have looked at a breakdown of costs for a
funeral? How many people have thought
about planning an alternative funeral that
meets their financial and psychological
needs? How many people know the
National Funeral Directors Association has
a hot-line for consumers to report any
abuse they encounter? (That number is 1-
800-662-7666.) For most people these
questions go unanswered until they are
faced with a death.

I was approached by a TV newswoman
doing a special on funerals. She wanted to
know if I knew of any bereaved who were
dissatisfied with the funeral home they had
chosen when their loved one died. I hadn't
come up against that problem among all
the bereaved I had met. The reporter said
she was doing a story about unscrupulous
funeral homes. I suggested she try a
different angle and do a positive story
about what the funeral industry is doing to

meet the changing times. This reporter typified the average sentiment that somehow the funeral industry is responsible for everything that is wrong with our death traditions. It seems as though the media are uncomfortable presenting a positive image of the funeral industry for fear they'll be accused of some unforgivable sin.

This book outlines many helpful suggestions and facts concerning the funeral.

Funeral Etiquette[1]

Should children be allowed to attend funerals?

One of the worst things adults can do is keep the death of a loved one a mystery to a child. The educational process about death begins in the home when children are young. If they are not exposed to the process, children are unlikely to be prepared for their own life losses.

Many funeral homes have children's slide shows or videos that explain death and what happens when a loved one dies. Special time is often set aside to show children these presentations before they view the deceased.

If you are uneasy and have questions or concerns about your little one attending a wake or funeral, discuss it with your funeral director or your clergyman. Usually, they will encourage you to expose your child to your rituals and traditions. They should have access to the many publications available on the subject written especially with children in mind.

One of the complaints most often heard from adults who have experienced the death of a loved one when they were children is how they were excluded from the funeral and arrangements. This usually occurred because their parents or relatives were uncomfortable with the loss and didn't know how to handle it themselves. They assumed that if they were having difficulty, a child certainly would not be able to cope.

Sixty percent of children between the ages of two and eight years who lose primary family members don't participate in the funeral rituals. Of course, participating in the service might not be appropriate for various reasons (a child should never be *made* to attend a funeral or wake), but it is important to introduce our traditions about death to children. It is an important part of their social and psychological growth. To deny them these lessons is to delay the inevitable.

One of the key issues in grief is accepting the finality of the death. There is no better way of doing this than going through the process of a wake and funeral, and children need a closure just as adults do. Children experience "magical thinking": They make up fantasies to help themselves cope. The wake and funeral experiences are often good ways to dispel many of the grief fantasies children create. Introducing children to death rituals is a normal and important part of their development.

ૐ

When my ex-husband's grandfather died, I brought my youngest son, age four, with me to the wake. He went right up to his great-grandfather's casket and touched his face, then asked me why he was so cold. My older son, who was seven years old at the time, wanted to go to the wake and I had said, "No." He was very close to his great grandfather.

I figured it wouldn't bother my younger son because he wouldn't know the difference, but that it would be too sad for the older boy. I guess I was the one with the "magical thinking" in those days.

My first experience at a wake was when I was eleven years old and my best friend died. I was scared to see her dead. My parents walked me into the dimly lit funeral parlor and there was Virginia. I remember screaming.

I would not forget that scene for a long time. A little preparation prior to visiting the funeral home might have helped me through this first funeral experience.

Is it normal to feel uncomfortable about going to a wake?

None of us wants to die. Getting in touch with our own feelings about our own death is not a common, everyday occurrence. Certainly attending a wake or funeral is not a pleasant experience, and it often brings up uncomfortable feelings about our own death.

Historically, wakes were used to keep a "watch" or "wake" over the deceased. This served two purposes: to psychologically condition friends and family to life without their loved one and to provide continued observation of the corpse in case it were to return to consciousness (premature burial).[2]

The old Jewish custom of "watching" or "waking" the dead was rooted in a genuine concern by relatives and friends that no person should be buried alive.

To ensure against such a terrible contingency the sepulcher was left unsealed for three days so that the corpse might be scrutinized frequently for signs of life.

This practice was taken over by the early Christians, who used the occasion to gather and say prayers for the repose of the deceased.[2]

Is it okay to wear colorful clothes to a funeral, or is black still considered the only appropriate color to wear?

Deciding on What Color to Wear to the Funeral

Traditionally in the United States dark colors (usually black) are worn during and

15

after a funeral, though brighter and lighter colors are showing up more and more often. Unless there is a religious significance (as in the Chinese-American rite, which calls for white), there is no need for the family or others to wear black.

❧

I wore a navy blue suit to the children's funeral. I'm not sure where it came from because all my clothes were burned in the fire.

Up until a few years ago my wardrobe consisted of black, gray, and brown. My sister, who is an interior designer, pointed this out to me one day. I was surprised. I was really not conscious that I was wearing only dark colors. It wasn't until I started feeling better inside that I started reflecting it outside, by wearing brighter, more vibrant colors.

A good friend of mine would not wear red after her daughter died. She had always considered red a "fun" color. She finally wore it at Christmas, a year after her daughter's death. For her, wearing red again was a statement of things getting back to normal.

Is it appropriate to bring a remembrance to be put in the casket of the deceased?

There is nothing wrong with bringing a remembrance to be buried with a loved one. If the casket is closed the funeral director will see to it that your remembrance is placed with the deceased at the time of burial.

❧

Many of my children's friends brought favorite toys or little trinkets and put them on top of the closed caskets of my children at their wake. I had never seen this done before. My niece brought her Pac Man watch for John John. He had always loved it.

A young man who was an avid hunter was killed in a farm accident. The family buried his favorite hunting gear with him. Maybe this tradition is carried down from the Egyptians who buried entire households in the pyramids to help the deceased in his new life.

How long should one stay at a wake?

Historically wakes lasted from eight hours to three days, depending on cultural and religious beliefs. Today, most wakes last for a couple of hours. A wake usually implies a visiting time set aside for friends and families to view the deceased and pay respects to the family. Perhaps for this reason the term now more frequently used is "visiting hours."

It is appropriate to visit, talk briefly with the family and then leave. Unless you are closely related or feel the need to stay, a ten or twenty-minute visit is usually long enough.

What is aftercare?

Seeking Help After the Funeral

Aftercare is a grief support network that has sprung up in funeral homes around the country. It is in response to the many survivors who have gone back to their funeral directors asking for help and guidance through their grief. Many bereaved today find themselves alone and without neighbors or religious support.

Because most funeral homes do not have professional grief counselors, they have developed unique ways to help the survivor. Some funeral homes offer space for local bereavement support groups to meet. Other funeral homes sponsor local support groups to meet in other locations. Some funeral homes (although few at this writing) have certified grief counselors on staff and offer individual grief counseling. Still other homes simply have a coffee on a Sunday afternoon and invite the recently bereaved to come. It is a time of sharing and exchanging information about how each person is coping and about local support groups.

There are special professional consulting groups, such as Accord in Kentucky, that conduct seminars to help funeral homes deal with this tremendous need. They offer, for example, special seminars near holidays, which are geared to help families deal with this emotionally charged time of year.[1]

Recently I conducted an aftercare program for a funeral home attended by about thirty people. Most of these people had lost a loved one within the past year. Before everyone arrived, the staff and I reviewed the different families so we could match widows with the widows, child losses with child losses, etc. For many of these people, it was a first time back to the funeral home since the death of their loved one. Not an easy thing to do. (It took me five years to go back to the funeral home that took care of the funeral arrangements for the children.)

We gave them information about local support groups and offered help with transportation if it was needed. One woman whose son had been murdered had not slept a full night in a year. We put her in touch with the local victim's rights group and she found support and understanding from people who could identify with her grief and suffering. They assisted her throughout the court case. She soon began to sleep through the night.

Two young children, ages ten and eleven, who lived across from the funeral home, had lost their six-month-old brother to Sudden Infant Death Syndrome, and two weeks later lost their grandfather who lived nearby. It was interesting to watch these children interact with the adults attending the coffee. The children spoke openly of their brother and grandfather. Age and death. Many adults spoke with these children about their feelings and vice versa. What a special afternoon that was.

As I saw different life stories walk into the funeral home that day, I thought about my own grief journey. For the first time I recognized the burden of making that journey without my spouse. Many of the couples who attended seemed solid and together. And although they had suffered as I had, they still had each other and, in most cases, other children. Most of the people in the group were quite religious. One woman in her mid seventies, who had lost children, spouse, and a grandchild, told me with her crystal clear eyes and beautiful vibrant face that Jesus was the answer and that he had seen her through much suffering — and much joy.

I've thought about that woman many times. For her the answer was Jesus. There was no question about that.

And still another woman who had lost her adult son told me that her surviving children and husband were her strength. Many of these people didn't need the long-term therapy I have had. This group reminded me that every grief situation is different and that each person develops his own coping mechanisms. This group was strong in faith and family. Although they'll never know it, they helped to renew my faith in life and most of all in myself.

Is it important that the funeral rite take place soon after the death of a loved one?

Whatever your death tradition, it should not be delayed because of business or weather. Years ago in cold climates if you died in the winter, your body was held in a crypt until spring. Nowadays, such delays are rarely required.

Timing of the Burial is Important

Some funerals today are postponed to fit the schedules of busy family members. However, postponing the funeral rite postpones the important process of grieving.

❧

An elderly woman and man – well into their eighties – lived together. Both had lost spouses and decided to spend their last years together. The gentleman died. His son, who is quite famous, called the funeral director to tell him to hold his father's body for six weeks because he was on a speaking tour and could not change his schedule.

The woman had to deal with her gentleman friend being held "in cold storage." She visited the funeral home weekly and asked to see her friend. Because they never married, she did not feel she had a right to interfere.

What is a memorial service?

A memorial service honors the deceased, although the body is not present. Today there are many different types of memorial services held in funeral homes, private homes, churches, favorite places of the deceased.

❧

Joan, age twenty-six, died at a Ronald McDonald House, where she had stayed during the last months of her life. Her family lived out of state so they were not familiar with the friends she had made there. A group of the volunteers who had grown close to Joan decided to have their own memorial service for her. They had a pot-luck dinner in her honor and taped their conversation. It was like a "roast," but done with love and respect. They sent the tape to Joan's family. Needless to say, the family was touched.

What appropriate ceremonies/ services exist for the non-religious people and their family and friends?

Non-religious funerals may be held at the funeral home or grave site with a funeral director or a close friend reading a eulogy. (In the old days this was frequently done at home.) The family of the deceased can plan the entire service with the help of the funeral director.

Even though a family has broken religious ties, are there instances where a member of the clergy will preside?

Most funeral directors will be more than helpful in retaining the services of a clergyman or rabbi. There are degrees of cooperation among clergymen and rabbis with regard to this issue. Your local funeral director is often your best resource because he knows the local clergy who will be available and sympathetic.

❦

At a funeral convention I attended, a funeral director told the story of a family who had requested the services of a minister. The minister arrived five minutes before the service was to begin and was briefed by the funeral director about the deceased and his family history. (You can imagine how little he was able to tell him in five minutes.) The minister walked into the viewing room, which had flower arrangements scattered around the casket. He noticed one arrangement had "AA" on a ribbon tied across the bouquet and assumed this meant Alcoholics Anonymous. He proceeded to give a twenty-minute eulogy on alcoholism. The AA stood for Athletic Association.

The funeral director who told this story suggested that it is better to have a family member, close friend, or funeral director give the eulogy if the clergyman is not familiar with the deceased or is not given proper time to prepare for the service.

The Eulogy Makes a Lasting Impression

Is it always appropriate to send flowers when a person dies?

It is important to check the obituary to find out the wishes of the family. Many times the obituary will specify no flowers and ask that donations be made to a specified charity. Don't ignore that wish. Culturally, for example, Orthodox Jews do not include flowers in their tradition.

❧

When my children died we asked in the obituary for donations for specific charities in honor of each child in place of flowers. However, many people sent flowers anyway (probably because some people lived away and did not read the obituary).

When I walked into the wake, there was a huge spray of black and white flowers in the formation of a keyboard in honor of my children's musical talents. It was beautiful and I could not get that picture out of my head for long time. I felt sick whenever I thought about it. It reminded me of my music, the children, and the fun we all had together. I wasn't ready to deal with that loss yet. I know it was intended to be a loving remembrance. It just didn't turn out that way. Whenever I send flowers now, I like to keep them simple.

Is it appropriate to bring food to the family of the deceased?

There probably isn't a longer-held tradition than bringing food to friends when there is a death. It has been the proverbial "ice breaker" for centuries. Dropping by with a special dish allows you the opportunity to visit for a moment and keep in touch with the bereaved.

It is important to be aware of the deceased's family's dietary customs. Rather than bringing the traditional cakes and pies, try to bring non-perishables and frozen food. Highly sugared foods are not good for anyone, including children.

❧

Many years ago a group from my church decided to help out a friend who had lost her husband. She had four children and worked full-time. After the funeral (when all too often friends stop calling and coming by) we started bringing dinner to her and her family. Each one of us was assigned a night for several weeks. These meals were appreciated by this woman and her family. Spreading your generosity and personal contact over a period of time is extremely important to the bereaved.

Viewing the Deceased

In the old days viewing the deceased was automatic. Why is there so much discussion about it today?

In the old days funerals were done at home. The family prepared the body and then it was laid out in the family parlor for viewing. Death was a family affair. Families spent time with the deceased right after death. Today many families do not spend that critical time saying good-bye to their loved one. For some, their next viewing is after the embalming, or there is no viewing at all. Most people who have experienced viewing a loved one immediately after death say that the experience left them with peaceful and tranquil memories of the deceased. This single experience often stays with the bereaved and is a consoling memory throughout the long grief process.

The trend today is to get the business of death over with as quickly as possible. Much of the responsibility for handling our dead has been given to the funeral director. However, viewing the deceased is as important a part of the grief process in our society as it ever was.

What happens to the deceased after the viewing (wake)?

A seventy-two-year-old woman had died and the family had just left the viewing room to get ready to go to the cemetery for the burial. I stayed behind with the staff. Mary showed me a small parchment paper that looked like a miniature scroll. On it was the history, from birth to death, of the deceased woman, the names of her children and important dates. It was done in calligraphy. Mary rolled this scroll up and placed it in a metal tube underneath the head of the deceased. I thought of a time capsule.

Arthur then took off the deceased's watch and rings and dropped them into my hands. He told me to put them in the office and make sure the family got them. As I stood holding those beautiful pieces of jewelry I wondered why I had always valued my possessions so much. There I was holding this stranger's very personal, life-long mementos, only to drop them into an envelope and give them to relatives. I felt peculiar that these cold pieces of jewelry somehow were untouched by this woman's death.

Arthur took off the woman's eyeglasses, put them in the eyeglass case and tucked them under her arm. As I watched him I was amazed by how he treated her with such gentleness and respect. He then covered her face and slowly closed the casket. I stood in awe. I saw this woman for the last time anyone would ever see her in this life. I felt privileged and yet saddened. I wanted to say, "Don't go yet!" But she was gone. I know someday that woman will be me.

Is it considered morbid to touch a deceased person?

Touching is not morbid. However, it is important to prepare someone for the experience. Realizing that a dead body will feel cold or hard is important. Often just seeing the nurse, doctor, or funeral director touching the body lets the family know it is okay.

Touching the Body is not Morbid

Will the deceased person look different in the casket than when he was alive?

Our own mythical thinking leads us to believe that someone can look as good dead as alive. As a culture we have encouraged the funeral industry to try its best to make death look like life. Often they do a good job, and sometimes they don't. We should remember the speed at which the body changes when death occurs.

Many people who are present at the moment of death of a loved one say they feel privileged because they saw death in its natural and peaceful state. It is often comforting for survivors who have seen a loved one suffer to finally see the peace that death brings.

≈

A good friend's mother died around 2 a.m. Mary got a call from her father to please go to the hospital. She went immediately. She told me her mother looked so peaceful and at rest in the hospital bed. The nurse told Mary her mother had asked for a wash cloth and comb just an hour before she had died. It was as if she was preparing herself. Mary said she was so glad she saw her mother like that because at the wake, after the embalming and make-up, her mother did not look as natural and peaceful.

Will a funeral home allow a family member to participate in washing or dressing the body?

Most funerals homes will be extremely cooperative in including family members who wish to participate in washing or dressing the body.

≈

I attended a workshop in which a woman shared the story of how she said good-bye to her mother when she died. Whenever the woman had gotten together with her mother she always curled her hair. When her mother died she asked the funeral director if she could fix her mother's hair one more time. Everyone in the family thought she was a little crazy, but the funeral director encouraged her and offered his help if she needed it.

The woman spent almost two hours fixing her mother's hair and talking to her. She said she didn't realize how straight hair becomes after death, so it took longer to arrange. While she was curling her mother's hair she found herself telling her mother, "Mom, you would just die if you saw the way your hair looks right now." She said her mother's hair wasn't perfect but would do. This final gesture gave her a memory she would always treasure.

If the casket is closed and you would like to view your friend, is it possible to do that?

Many families prefer a closed casket but are not against allowing friends to view. Always ask the funeral director if you feel the need to see your friend. He will do his best to get you that permission.

Is it appropriate to take a picture or video of the deceased and/or the funeral?

Taking Pictures and Videos at Funerals

It is appropriate for families to video tape as well as take photographs of the deceased. Pictures and videos allow the bereaved to recall exactly the events surrounding the funeral. Many cultures use the deceased's picture on memorial and remembrance cards.

Some hospitals will take pictures of stillborns. This might seem a little morbid for people who have never had a stillborn child, but these pictures may become valuable mementos to the surviving family.

Videos provide survivors with one-hundred-percent recall of the event and children who are not present an opportunity to view the funeral. It is used also for elderly family members who might not be physically able to attend the funeral. Do not discourage a friend or family member from having a picture or video taken because you are not comfortable with the idea.

What are the recent trends in traditional funerals being held in the United States?

In recent years there has been a decline in the number of traditional funerals. (By "traditional" we mean a wake, service, and burial.) Many people opt for cremation and skip the traditional funeral. It is not uncommon to read in obituaries that services will be held privately and are only for the immediate family.

The problem with this trend is that it is eliminating one of the few opportunities most people have to express their grief at the time of a death. Funerals are a way of honoring the deceased, but more important they are for the living. (One recent survey revealed that forty-five percent of funeral-goers attend for their own comfort, and eighteen percent attend to honor the deceased.) Allowing the community to express its grief and show its respect is important for the community as well as the grieving family. A public funeral gives everyone permission to grieve.

Many people want to hurry up the funeral rituals. They seem to feel that once they get "it" over with everything will be back to normal. Of course, that doesn't work. Many bereaved have traced their unresolved grief back to the time of the funeral. Much to their surprise, they find many questions about the funeral that they cannot answer: Why didn't they view the body? What was their loved one wearing? Why didn't they have a public wake? Who made certain decisions about the funeral?

How do funeral directors deal with family feuds and affairs of the deceased?

Managing Family Feuds During Funerals

It is important to inform the funeral director of any affairs or family feuds that might be currently on the agenda at the time of the deceased's death. Sometimes it seems funeral directors should wear a whistle to referee the family problems that arise when such dynamics come into play.

A balance must be struck between the grief of, for example, a separated wife and the current lover of a deceased. Funeral directors need to be informed of all situations however embarrassing they may be in order to do the right thing for everyone concerned. Most funeral directors are experts at diplomacy and have handled just about every situation you can imagine.

At the time of our children's funeral, my husband and I had been separated for six months and had filed for divorce. He chose to bring his girlfriend to the wake and funeral. I was alone. Many people asked me how I felt about his girlfriend being so visible, standing as she did in the front row at the funeral Mass. I didn't really think much about it. It is funny with death: certain things just don't matter anymore.

Both sides of the family were thrown together at a very emotional and sorrowful time. The young cousins were shocked and couldn't begin to understand what all this meant. They really didn't understand divorce, let alone death.

My sisters were divorced, and their ex-husbands were there, including some of their parents. Extended families. There was no Emily Post advice for this gathering.

Funeral Arrangements

Is it important for the whole family to be involved in making funeral arrangements?

It is extremely important that everyone participate and make his wishes known for the funeral of the loved one. Even children should be involved. There is a natural tendency to want to spare a distraught spouse or elderly parent from this chore. Remember that participating in the planning of the funeral is part of the healing process. It isn't always comfortable, but it is necessary.

Sometimes a funeral director will go to the home of the family. This all depends on many circumstances. Most often the funeral is planned in the funeral home. It takes at least two hours to make the arrangements. It is during this time a casket and vault are chosen.

આ

I remember walking into the funeral home and asking the funeral director for a pack of cigarettes. I hadn't smoked in a long time. He asked my husband and me if we wanted to view the children. We looked at each other and said no. I will regret that decision the rest of my life.

I sat at a round table with a bunch of people. All I remember is that someone asked us what we wanted listed in the obituary for charities. Someone at the table wanted money donated to the local high school. I said I wanted the monies to go for organizations in which the children were involved — the skating association, music department and the ski association. That is all I remember. I don't recall picking out caskets or vaults or discussing the arrangements. However, I was present at the table, so all of these things must have been decided.

I do remember thinking after it was all over that I had hoped we had gotten the best caskets for the children. After all, they would never be going to college or anything. That kind of logic isn't uncommon when you're grieving.

How do you pay for a funeral?

There are many different ways to pay for a funeral. Some funeral homes allow time payments, others require the money up front, still others take Mastercard or VISA. And of course, most funeral homes and cemeteries offer pre-arrangement programs for people to take care of all arrangements before the death of a loved one or themselves. However they are paid for, funerals cost quite a bit of money.

It is extremely important that spouses have joint accounts, so if one dies, the other has access to monies to help pay the expenses of the funeral. The average cost for a funeral in 1991 was $4,253.11, with no marker or cemetery lot. Most people do not keep thousands of dollars of available cash in their checking accounts. So savings accounts should be accessible to either spouse.

What is the procedure for making a typical funeral arrangement?

Once you have chosen the funeral director you will set up a time to make the arrangements. It is usually the funeral director who will pick up the body and bring it to the funeral home. (It is smart to be thinking now who you would use.)

*Making the
Funeral
Arrangements*

Do not be afraid to discuss prices with funeral directors. They will itemize all their services and products. Their bills include rental time for the wake and even rental of the casket if the deceased will be cremated after the viewing.

They offer many different models of caskets, urns, and vaults. The fee can run anywhere from $500 to the thousands. It's like buying a car. If you want the Cadillac of caskets, it is available.

Whatever you decide, it is important to have a second party along who is not emotionally involved with the loss. She can ask questions in case you are unable to. As cold as it might sound, you need to decide on your budget for the funeral.

Again, in 1991, the average funeral averaged about $4,300, which does not include the cost of a cemetery lot or gravestone marker.

Following is a list of items to be discussed and decided upon during the arrangements:
- Select clergy
- Select music and organist
- Decide if hairdresser is needed and any other cosmetic considerations the funeral director will need to know if there is to be a viewing of the body.
- Discuss what the deceased will wear and bring to the funeral home

- Decide what personal effects will be left on the deceased (jewelry, etc.)
- Open or closed casket
- Time of visiting hours if there is a wake
- Cemetery lot purchased
- Clear funeral time with church
- Select pallbearers
- Select casket or urn
- Arrange police escort
- Order vault
- Write newspaper obituary and funeral notice
- Order flowers
- File insurance papers if applicable
- Purchase copies of death certificates (at least a half-dozen to use in filing insurance and other important papers)

Besides this, the funeral director will:
- File the embalmer's affidavit
- Obtain burial permit
- Obtain death certificates
- File the death certificates
- Notify Social Security
- Obtain Veterans Administration (VA) flag when applicable
- File VA allowance application when applicable
- Prepare memorial folder (Mass card etc.)
- File application for VA headstone when applicable

- Notify Department of Social Welfare when applicable
- Notify crematory when applicable
- Transport body for post-mortem if called for
- Embalm and prepare body

Getting an Idea of the Costs

What is a bill for a typical, traditional funeral?

These bills do not include purchasing a cemetery lot, headstone or marker.

Note: This is an actual bill taken from a funeral home in New England in June 1992.

Services:

Removal of body from Home or Hospital	$ 75
Embalming	200
Additional Preparation (Hair)	50
Arrangements and Direction of Funeral	350
Secure Legal Documents	25
SUBTOTAL	700

Facilities:

Preparation Room	50
Memorial Home and Staff	390
Church or Home Service	300
Visiting Hours (Public)	250
SUBTOTAL	990

Motor Vehicles:

Service Car for Removal	75
Funeral Coach (Hearse)	125
Limo	50
SUBTOTAL	250

Merchandise:

Casket	1,095
Vault	735
Clothing	25
Guest Register	25
SUBTOTAL	1,880

Estimated Cash Advances:

Clergy	50
TOTAL	$3,870

Items which are listed under "Services" provided by the funeral home staff are less expensive in rural areas, while products listed under "Merchandise" (like caskets and vaults) are less costly in metropolitan areas.

Because of a Federal Trade Commission ruling several years ago, funeral homes must give a breakdown of prices for every bill presented. This was brought about in an attempt to keep the abuses in the industry to a minimum. (Financial Operations Survey 1985 NFDA)

What is a bill for a "no frills" cremation?

Note: This is an actual bill taken from a funeral home in New England in 1992.

Services

Transfer body from home or hospital	$ 75
Embalming	200
Additional preparation (hair)	50
Arrangements and direction of funeral	150
Secure legal documents	25
Removal to crematorium	75
SUBTOTAL	575

Embalming is not a legal requirement. It is, however, a requirement of _____ Memorial Home.

Facilities:

Preparation Room	$50
Memorial home and staff	200
Private viewing family only	100
SUBTOTAL	350

Motor Vehicles:

Service car for removal	75
Service car to crematorium	75
SUBTOTAL	150

Merchandise:

Cremation container	100

Estimated cash advances:

Cremation charge	165
Medical Examiner Permit	10
SUBTOTAL	175
TOTAL	$1,350

Personal Note: I did not include one of the $599 cremation specials that are offered in certain parts of the country because of my belief in the traditional funeral and its benefit to the grief process. The above bill does minimize costs but still includes family viewing and visitation time, critical to the grief process.

What is a bill for a cremation with a regular funeral service?

The Cost of a Cremation with Funeral Service

Note: This is an actual bill taken from a funeral home in Vermont.

Services

Transfer body to funeral home	$ 60.00
Service car	75.00
Embalming	275.00
Arrangements	550.00
Preparation room	90.00
Use of funeral home	385.00
Flower car	75.00
SUBTOTAL	1,510.00

Merchandise

Casket rental (for viewing)	575.00
Urn	325.00
Vault for urn	175.00
SUBTOTAL	1,075.00

Cash Advanced:

Flowers	150.00
Organist	35.00
Hairdresser	100.00
Crematory fee	225.00
Newspaper notice	142.80
Burial Permit	10.00
Death Certificates (2 copies)	10.00
SUBTOTAL	672.80
TOTAL DUE	$3,257.80

Funeral Directors

Do funeral directors and embalmers need to be licensed? What type of education do they have?

Each state has its own licensing requirements. All require a state exam and an apprenticeship in a funeral home. The average apprenticeship is about twelve months. Many states require two years of college as a prerequisite for taking the exam. There are two separate exams, one for funeral director and one for embalmer.

Fifty percent of funeral directors/embalmers hold college degrees, and more than seventy-five percent have had formal education in funeral service.

Are funeral homes unionized?

Less than two percent of funeral homes are unionized. Six states currently have unions: Indiana, Illinois, Michigan, Minnesota, New Jersey and New York; the District of Columbia is also unionized.

Embalming

Is embalming a legal requirement in most states?

Only twenty states require embalming - and then, only under certain circumstances:
1) the body is to be transported by common carrier;
2) the body is not to be buried within forty-eight hours;
3) the deceased died of a communicable disease.

Then why do most funeral homes require embalming?

Many funeral directors require embalming for reasons of sanitation. They also feel it allows the family to experience a more pleasant viewing of the deceased.

Why Funeral
Homes Require
Embalming
With most families scattered across the country, funerals are often delayed at least twenty-four to forty-eight hours until family members arrive.

Embalming is not new in many cultures around the world, but is it is relatively new in the United States. The practice started in the late nineteenth century and has only been used widely since the 1920s.

It has become an integral part of the funeral service and is relatively inexpensive (the average charge for an embalming is $200).

Cremation

How many cremations are done in a year in the United States?

According to the Cremation Association of North America, in 1884 there were 41 cremations in the United States; in 1991 there were 376,975 cremations (17.02 percent of the total 2,162,000 deaths).

Do you make arrangements for a cremation the same way you do for a traditional funeral?

Although the arrangements will vary according to budget, as in any traditional funeral, the family can choose a traditional service with viewing and church services. There are cemeteries, scatter gardens and vaults for cremains (the term used to refer to the ashes of the deceased).

Niches are enclosed shelves in a mausoleum that allow the family to come and view the urn. Only eighteen percent of families keep the cremains in their own possession.

A recent study, Project Understanding NFFS, shows which options for disposition of cremains are most used nationwide:

Bury Ashes – 38%
Niche or Tomb – 15%
Scatter Ashes – 27%
Family Possession – 18%
Undecided (Usually left at funeral
   home) – 2%

❧

Bob, who manages a chain of funeral homes in California, which does 10,000 funerals a year (4,000 of which are cremations), speaks about the importance of giving people alternatives for burial of ashes. He tells the story about a woman whose daughter had died. The mother came back to the funeral home some two years later quite upset about the decision to scatter her daughter's ashes. She said she was not given any other option for the ashes other than scattering and really missed not having a place to visit her daughter. Bob righted the situation the best he could by having a brass plate made and placing it in one of the remembrance gardens. This woman then had a place to go to in memory of her daughter.

Bob suggests that funeral homes give people thirty days to think about scattering. He says more than half of the clients come back and decide against it because they like to have a place to visit their loved one.

Does a cremation affect the grief process?

Many funeral directors have told me that some families have difficulty picking up the cremains.*

The reality of seeing the ashes of their loved one in an urn is disturbing to some Americans, though it is traditional in many other cultures.

This discomfort has led to a problem: A significant number of families simply leave the cremains at the funeral home. Most states have laws that prohibit the disposal of human remains, including ashes, without permission, and others are passing statutes permitting funeral homes to dispose of unclaimed cremains after a specified time period (e.g.: Florida 120 days).

⽑

I attended a memorial service of a dear
and wonderful woman who had taken
care of my sister's children. When we
walked in the funeral home, I saw an urn
in the front of the room. It was my first
experience with a cremation, and I found
it difficult to think of Margaret in terms of
ashes. I also had trouble with the size of
the urn. This is probably because my
cultural upbringing did not include
cremations. With the increase of
cremations in our country, I think many
people will become comfortable with it as
a logical option for disposition of the
dead.

I think the question of having a place to
memorialize the deceased is the main
issue for the survivors. Although some
people are comfortable with scattering,
many more need a place to go and visit
their loved ones.

How long does a cremation take and what is the process?

Some cremations take only an hour,
others up to three and a half hours.
Depending upon the size of the deceased
and the type of container used, an average
cremation will take about one an a half
hours.

It takes some time for the chamber to cool down after the cremation. At this point the ashes, which weigh from three to seven pounds, are removed. The crematory then separates any foreign matter with an electromagnet.

The ashes (which really are leftover bone fragments) are put through a pulverizer and ground to a fine consistency. They are then packaged in temporary containers and shipped to their destination, usually the funeral home.

Burial and Cemetery

Do cemeteries require that a vault be used for a burial?

Most cemeteries today require the use of a vault. Vaults keep the earth from settling in after the burial. However, there are no state statutes governing the use of vaults.

Vaults are usually made of concrete, metal or fiberglass. An average vault costs $500.

Do people still dig graves by hand?

Many graves are still hand dug. The charge for opening and closing a grave ranges from $150 on up, depending on the region of the country.

(In Vermont it costs about $200 to open and close a grave. In Florida it costs between $250-$550 for the same service.)

Some Graves are Still Dug By Hand

While I attended a friend's funeral, I asked the funeral director what would happen after everyone left the funeral. He invited me to stay behind and meet the grave diggers and vault people. I had never really thought about anyone digging graves. Sure enough, as the last funeral car pulled away, a truck with a woman and a man in it pulled up. When they approached us I noticed the woman wearing a T-shirt that read, "Kiss my ass I'm on vacation." The man was a dead look-alike of Darrell on *The Newhart Show*. The woman turned out to be the major caretaker for this beautiful little cemetery. She spoke of each person buried as if he/she were family. As I watched her fill the grave, I was impressed by how perfectly symmetrical the grave was. I could see the vault of the deceased's husband (he had died twelve years before) within inches of the one being dug. I thought of a pastry chef. This here grave digging was a work of art!

Next a huge truck with two young boys hanging out the back pulled up with the vault cover. They proceeded to take the awning and artificial turf away. They lowered the casket. The young boys were helping their father. It was business as usual. I asked questions and they answered. I was the uncomfortable one, not they. The vault man told me there are waterproof vaults and ones that aren't. I asked him what difference it made. He said many people want to know that their loved one will not get wet, especially if the grave is near an underground stream. I listened. He told me that once the vault cover was put in place it was permanently sealed.

Meanwhile the grave digger told me she was a professional organist and taught music. "Darrell" never said anything. Just shoveled dirt into the grave.

I drove back to the funeral home feeling that all this business at the grave site was very normal and wondered why all these years I had this fear about what went on in cemeteries.

What is the cost of a lot in a cemetery?

Cemetery lots cost anywhere from $200 up. A deed to the lot is issued at the time of the purchase. Usually families purchase several adjacent lots so they will be guaranteed space together.

Who owns cemeteries?

Most cemeteries are owned by a church, synagogue or municipality. However, today there is a trend toward privately owned cemeteries. Funeral homes may own cemeteries, although most do not.

Many large funeral corporations purchase cemeteries with on-site chapels, mausoleums, and crematoriums.

In certain areas of the country, people purchase what the industry calls "private family estates." These are several lots together. In Newport Beach, Calif., estates can have a view of the ocean and cost as much as $100,000 for traditional burials, or up to $60,000 for the burial of cremains.

I bought two lots next to my children's graves as did my ex-husband. We paid around $600 for these four lots in a beautiful cemetery overlooking Lake Champlain in Vermont.

Who takes care of maintaining a cemetery?

Whoever owns the cemetery takes care of maintenance. Many lots in cemeteries today are fully endowed with perpetual care. Perpetual care means that the care of the cemetery grounds is paid for when you purchase the lot and that the grounds will be maintained for the life of the cemetery. Other cemeteries do not offer perpetual care and charge an annual fee for maintenance. It is important to find out the annual cost of maintenance if perpetual care is not offered.

Ordering the Grave Stone or Marker

Where do you order a monument or marker for the grave site?

Certain businesses specialize in monuments and markers. You can pick out an in-stock monument or special order one. You may design your own monument including size, shape, and engraving.

Markers and gravestones are usually made of marble, granite, or bronze.

I had a nine-foot granite base made for the children engraved with the words, "The Ducham Children." Three standard-sized monuments stand on top of the base. The one for Johnette was in the shape of a heart. I had a drawing etched on each stone so children visiting the cemetery would know which stone belonged to which child. David John had the baseball and bat, John Peter had the hockey stick and puck, and Johnette had the piano keyboard.

My husband and I had a difficult time purchasing the stones. I do not like to go to the cemetery, but many people find it comforting and helpful.

We paid about $3,600 in 1983 for the three stones, including the base and installation. Around $300 for the three lots, plus the funeral charge, which was around $5,900 for the three children. Total was around $9,800.

What is a mausoleum?

The term "mausoleum" comes from the fourth-century B.C. Asia Minor King Mausolus. It means a "magnificent tomb." It is always above ground and is usually made of marble, stone, or granite.

Many people prefer to be buried this way because they consider it cleaner than an earth burial. A mausoleum can hold hundreds of caskets or can be erected for an individual.

How much you will pay for a mausoleum space depends in part on the level at which the casket is located. The large mausoleums usually have several levels, all at different price range. Certain levels are associated respectively with the heart and the eye and as such are the most expensive.

How soon after a burial should the grave marker or tombstone be placed?

Most cemeteries have no restrictions regarding when a marker should be placed. However, some religions have their own customs. Judaism marks the first anniversary of a death with the unveiling of the gravestone.

Many cemeteries mark the grave or niche with a temporary marker with the deceased's name on it because the family frequents the cemetery in the first few months after the death.

Investigating Alternatives to Cemeteries

Is a cemetery the only place the deceased can be legally buried?

Although extremely uncommon in this day, home burials are allowed. One needs to check state law and local zoning ordinances for rules regarding home burials.

Lisa Carlson suggests in her book *Caring for Your Own Dead,* "a family should consider the long-range implications on land value in (performing a home burial) because a graveyard becomes a permanent easement on the property in many states." She cites a 1959 Oklahoma case, Heiligman vs. Chambers, in which a grandson sued a new landowner to prevent him from removing the grandson's forbearers from the family cemetery although the deceased's heirs no longer owned the land.

The grandson won. The court in that state upheld "the right to permanency created by any such family burial ground."

Practical Questions About Funerals

How does one pre-pay for a funeral?

Prearranging one's own funeral is common in the United States. People have chosen to prearrange for several reasons, including:
1. Dealing with difficult decisions beforehand, not in a grief state.
2. Letting your wishes be known before you die.
3. Relieving family of financial burden.
4. Locking-in today's prices for tomorrow's funeral.

Prearrangement is very much like arranging a funeral at the time of death. One major difference is the funding vehicle. How to pay for it? Most prearrangements are funded with annuities, life insurance policies, savings accounts, bank trusts or other types of funding vehicles. However, each state has its own laws regulating prearrangement funding. It is important that you fully understand the funding arrangements before you sign any contracts.

Questions you should ask:

- How is it funded?
- What is the relationship between the entity providing the funding and the funeral home?
- What are the tax considerations?
- Are you purchasing a guaranteed funeral (regardless of the retail price of the funeral at the time of death, there would be no obligation to pay additional money to the funeral provider)?
- What are non-guaranteed contracts?
- Is this guarantee limited if you make installment payments as a method of payment?
- What if you relocate? Does your prearrangement contract work in another state?
- What are the penalties for cancellation of any changes in assignment, beneficiary designation or use of funds?
- What would be the impact on your funeral arrangement if you need to qualify for Medicaid and Social Security Income? (Both Medicaid and SSI allow a person to exclude prearranged funerals within certain limits.)

The Funeral Service Consumer Assistance Program (FSCAP), (not a legal entity or a funeral home or pre-need contract "rating" service), provides help in resolving problems and complaints concerning funeral homes. It also provides help in reviewing different prearrangement contracts. Some helpful questions to ask a sales counselor when inquiring about prearrangement from FSCAP:

Important Questions You Should Ask

- "More than half the states now require a license or permit to sell prearrangements contracts. Does this state? If so, what is your license number?"
- "I understand that virtually all states have a controlling agency that regulates the sale of these contracts. What is the name, address and phone of the one in this state?"
- "What if we need the services of two funeral homes, one in this state and one out-of-state? Why is there a need for two separate bills?"
- "If we change our minds after we sign, what is our time limit to cancel? What if we choose to cancel well after the time limit has expired?"
- "Is there any other vital information I need to know about possible additional charges, documents I'll need, the cemetery purchase, gravesite

charges or ground/air transportation? Have I asked every question? If I haven't, have you volunteered all the information you need to ensure satisfaction for me and my family?"

- "Does the cemetery plot meet the requirements of my religion?"
- "Are there any restrictions on the types of monuments and burial vaults I can choose?"
- "Does the price include perpetual care and maintenance?"
- "Are there other plots available in the same location to provide for the burial of my family?"

This information was provided, in part by the National Funeral Directors Association.

For more information, call FSCAP: 1-800-662-7666.

Does a veteran have funeral benefits available at the time of his death?

The following information is from the Code of Federal Regulations 1991. Title 38 VA benefits. U.S. Department of Veterans Affairs:

"Burial Benefits and Plot Allowances
"Veterans who die as a result of a service-connected disability are entitled to

a maximum of $1,500 for burial and funeral expenses, including the cost of transporting the body to the national cemetery nearest their home.

"Veterans who die for reasons other than service-connected disabilities on or after Oct. 1, 1981, may be entitled to up to $300 in burial benefits. Eligibility is established if the veteran

Veterans Benefits

- was entitled at the time of death to pension or compensation;
- died while hospitalized or domiciled in a VA facility or other facility at VA expense.

"For a death occurring on or after Nov. 30, 1990, an additional plot or interment allowance of up to $150 is available to the same categories of veterans eligible for the $300 burial benefits, and to those who are discharged or retired from service because of disability which incurred or was aggravated in the line of duty. Veterans of any war who died prior to Nov. 30, 1990, were also eligible for the plot allowance. The plot allowance is provided only for veterans who are not buried in a national cemetery.

"Claims for VA burial benefits must generally be filed within two years of permanent burial or cremation. Additional costs of transporting a body may be allowed if the veteran died at a VA hospital or other facility at VA expense, or if the veteran died in transit at VA expense to or from a medical facility. Members of the Reserves and the Army and Air National Guard who die while performing or as a result of active duty for training may also be eligible for burial benefits.

"Either the funeral director or the individual paying the burial expenses may claim reimbursement for burial and plot allowances through any VA office.

"Burial in National Cemeteries

"Eligibility for burial in a VA national cemetery is based on the length of time in active military service, and the nature of the veteran's separation from the service.

"Burial in a VA national cemetery is also available to an eligible veteran's spouse, widow or widower who has not remarried, minor children, and under certain circumstance, unmarried adult children."

A pamphlet titled *Interments in National Cemeteries*, available from VA regional offices, provides detailed information on national cemetery burial arrangements.

Be advised that Arlington National Cemetery is under the jurisdiction of the Department of the Army, not the Department of Veterans Affairs. With the exception of cremated remains, burial is limited to specific categories of military personnel and veterans. Write to the Superintendent, Arlington National Cemetery, Arlington, VA 22211, or call (202) 695-3253 or 3250.

For further information on government-provided markers, headstone, grave, or memorial markers (for any veteran whose remains were not recovered) contact: Director, Monument Service (42), National Cemetery System, Department of Veterans Affairs, Washington, D.C. 20420. Or call (202) 275-1494 or 1495.

Does Social Security provide benefits for burial and funeral expenses?

If you have worked and contributed to Social Security and leave a surviving spouse or dependent child, the allowance is $255.

What happens to the homeless and those without funds for burial?

The state social welfare office or the local municipality in which the death occurred provides some funds, varying substantially from location to location, for burial. Each locality has different laws regarding the amount of compensation.

It is not uncommon that monies allocated for the homeless do not provide for a regular burial and funeral. Often, there is just enough for a public burial. The following excerpt describes the burial of the homeless in the largest and most wealthy city in the United States.

Jonathan Kozol writes in *Rachel and Her Children*, about Potter's Field on Hart's island in Long Island Sound, New York City's public burial ground. He tells us that burials are done by prison inmates living on the island:

"The unembalmed bodies are taken in rough wooden boxes by the truckload from the hospital morgues. Twenty to thirty boxes, costing thirty-seven dollars each, are buried at one time in trenches. The boxes are stacked three deep and two across. There are no grave markers. After thirty or forty years, the graves are bulldozed to make room for more."

"Between 1981 and 1984, nearly half the children who died in New York City before their second year of life were buried at Potter's Field. Almost a third of all persons buried at Potter's field during those years were infants."

Footnotes

1 – (page 12, 19): *Death Etiquette for the '90s :What to Do/ What to Say;* Hartnett, J.; 1993.

2 – (pages 13, 15): *History of American Funeral Directing;* Habenstein, R.W.; 1962.

References

Aries, P. (1981). The hour of our death. New York: Oxford University Press.

Aries, P. (1974). Western attitudes toward death. Baltimore; The Johns Hopkins University Press.

Stephenson, J.S. (1985). Death, grief, and mourning. New York: The Free Press.

DeSpelder, L.A., & Strickland, A.L. (1987). The last dance. 2nd ed. California: Mansfield Publishing Co.

Rando, T.A. (1984). Grief, dying and death. Illinois: Research Press.

Kastenbaum, R.J. (1991). Death, society and human experience. New York: Merrill/Macmillan Publishing Co.

Marks, A.S. & Calder, B. (1982). Attitudes toward death and funerals. Illinois: Northwestern University.

Morgan, E. (1984). Dealing creatively with death. North Carolina: Celo Press.

Carlson, L. (1987). Caring for your own dead. Vermont: Upper Access.

Prepare yourself for one of the most difficult jobs you'll ever have: Grief.

If your bookstore or employer does not have the other books in this series, please indicate which ones and how many you need on the form below; cost of each book is $6.95, or $29.95 for the set.

Good Mourning also publishes a set of sympathy note cards (and envelopes) with artwork designed by children who have died. Included is a bookmark with suggested messages of sympathy, to facilitate your own written expression of sympathy to the bereaved – a poignant and personal way to express your sympathy. The cost of a set of 12 note cards/bookmarks is $9.95, plus postage and handling. Please send a check or money order for the total to:

Good Mourning
P.O. 9355
South Burlington, VT 05407-9355

Name of Book	Quantity	Each	Price
Using Grief to Grow: A Primer *How You Can Help/How to Get Help*		$6.95	
Different Losses Different Issues: *What to Expect and How to Help.*		$6.95	
The Funeral: An Endangered Tradition *Making Sense of the Final Farewell*		$6.95	
Grief in the Workplace: *40 Hours Plus Overtime*		$6.95	
Children and Grief: *Big Issues for Little Hearts*		$6.95	
Death Etiquette for the '90s: *What to Do/ What to Say*		$6.95	
Set of Six Books		$29.95	
Note Cards (one dozen, plus envelopes)		$9.95	
Subtotal			
Tax, if applicable			
Shipping/handling ($2.25 ea/$8 set)			
Total (check enclosed)			

Phone: 802-658-5883

Ship to:

*Name*_____

*Address*_____

*City*_____*State*_____*ZIP*_____

If you would like to submit a question regarding the death of a loved one, or learn how to support a friend who has lost a loved one, please do so in the space below or on your paper. I will be happy to respond to as many questions as I can.

With warmest regards, Johnette Hartnett

_____

_____

_____

_____

_____

_____

_____

_____

_____

_____

_____

_____

_____

_____

_____

_____

_____

_____

_____

_____

_____

_____